WHO surprised WHO?!

Written & illustrated by: Kathleen Mincer

Copyright © 2009 by Kathleen Mincer
Book design by Angela Mincer

Unless otherwise noted all scripture is taken from the New American Standard Bible (NASB)

Copyright 1960, 1962, 1963, 1968, 1971, 1972, 1973 1975,1977, 1995 by The Lockman Foundation

*Other versions used:
___Amplified Bible (AMP)
Copyright 1954, 1958, 1962, 1964, 1965, 1987 by The Lockman Foundation
___New Living Translation (NLT)
Holy Bible. New Living Translation Copyright 1996, 2004 by Tyndale Charitable Trust

MMMM

MODERN MIRACLES FOR MINI AND MAXI READERS

In the Old Testament God's people were told to build memorials so they would not forget what God had done for them. The following story is true. It is my personal "modern day memorial" in remembrance of how God proved Himself to me. The date was 1977 and the setting Indianapolis, Indiana; only the names have been changed. -KM

Audrey hated moving! Packing boxes and then turning around and unpacking them was definitely not her "cup of tea!" Audrey and her husband Mark, were in the process of moving into a new house. Well…it wasn't new, just new to them! The church where Mark worked was furnishing the house as part of his salary.

The house just suited Audrey! Upstairs it had three bedrooms: the first one was for Audrey & Mark; the second for their twin daughters, Jasmine & Jessica (who were almost seven); and the third bedroom was for their son, Justin (who was just barely five).

The kitchen, dining, and living rooms were downstairs. In the back of the house was a family room, plus a large additional bonus room. Audrey was excited about the bonus room. The previous owner had used it for an insurance office, but Audrey had something else in mind.

The bonus room would be perfect for a playroom! The children could have their own private place to play, and they wouldn't have to put their toys away every evening. If unexpected company showed up, the front of the house would still be clean…this was a mother's dream!

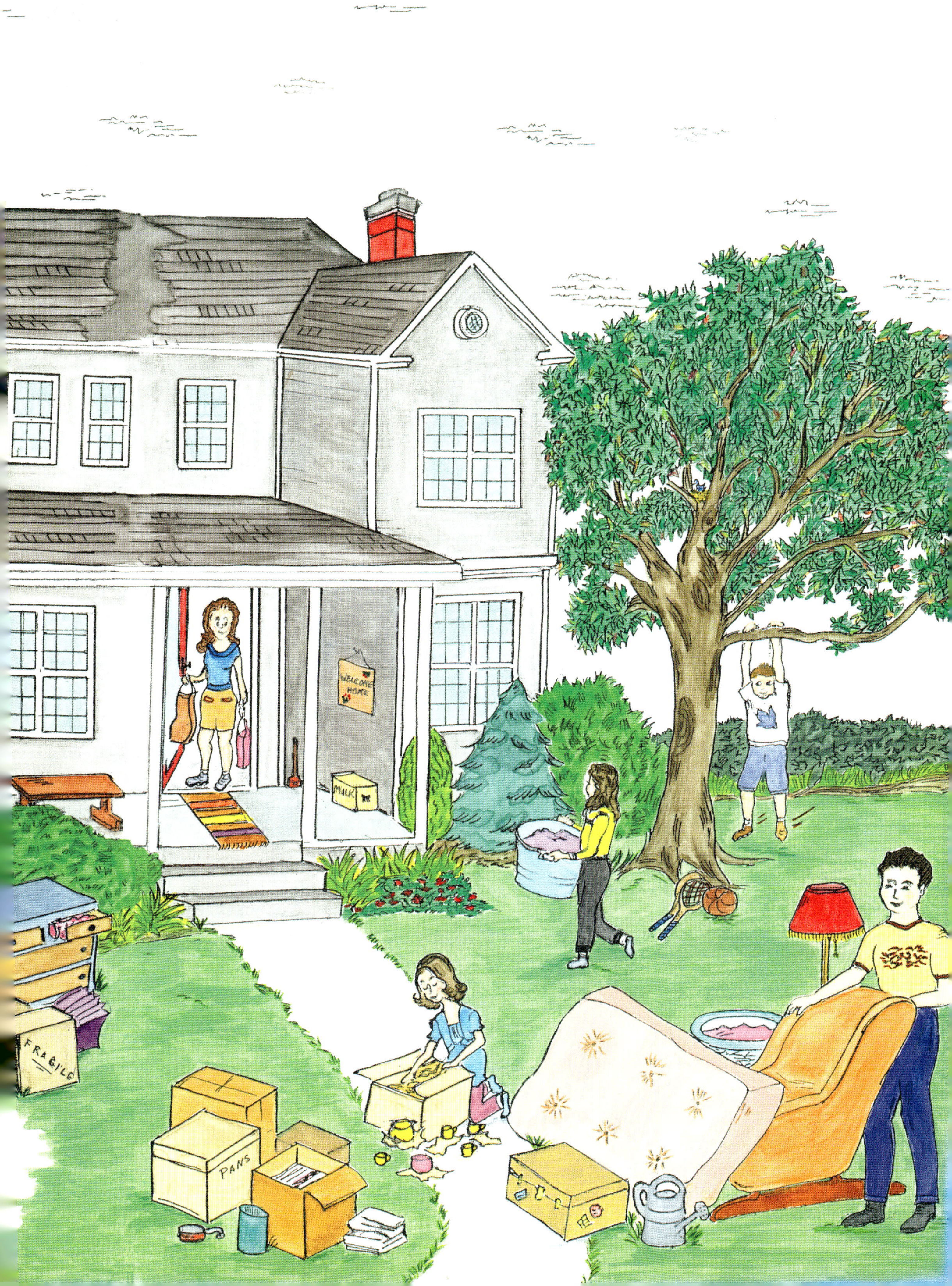
WELCOME HOME
MILK
FRAGILE
PANS

Mark worked for a large inner-city church, where he served as principal of their Christian school. Because the church employed a large staff, there was only so much money to go around. Audrey's choice to be a stay-at-home Mom made "the pickings even slimmer."

It wasn't long until Audrey had the house all cleaned up and everything put away. But the lack of money to use for any of her projects soon began to get Audrey down. Noticing Audrey's dilemma, her friend Carla loaned Audrey some teaching tapes. "Check these out." Carla said, "These tapes should cheer you up!"

Audrey's spirits lifted as she listened to the minister on the tapes talk about the love of God and how it was God's desire to bless His children. The minister quoted Jesus in John 16:23b & 24.

Truly, truly, I say to you, If you ask the Father for anything in My name, He will give it you. Until now you have asked nothing in My name: Ask, and you will receive, so that **your joy may be full.**

Was God really a caring Father who loved to bless His children?

___As a mother, there was nothing Audrey loved more, than to be able to give her children something they desired and see their eyes light up with joy!

___If it were true that God loved to bless His children, Audrey knew exactly what would bring the most joy to her. First and foremost, she wanted to fix up the bonus room into a playroom for the kids!

Audrey dreamed of making the playroom look like a miniature little house the children could call their own. In her imagination, she visualized the little house having a living room, a bedroom, and a kitchen…complete with a stove, refrigerator, and sink. There was plenty of old furniture that could be used for the living room and bedroom.

However, Audrey would need money to buy the stove, refrigerator, and sink. The little toy appliances stood three or four feet tall and were miniature models of the real thing. New, they cost about $20 apiece, which would be $60 for all three!

Audrey knew $60 was more than they could afford. Perhaps, she reasoned, she could find used ones at a garage sale or in the classified section of the local newspaper where used toys are advertised.

Nagging questions soon began to trouble Audrey. Is God really that interested in the everyday affairs of His children's lives? Would it be OK to ask Jesus for something so insignificant as toy kitchen appliances? Audrey had do admit, she had no idea.

Audrey remembered back to when she was a teenager. She had been bothered for weeks with terrible shooting pains up and down her right side. When the pain did not go away but instead got worse, her parents called their minister to come pray for her. After the minister prayed, the pain left…never to come back again. Talk about relieved and grateful!

But that was different from this?

___Didn't a situation have to be a life and death matter, before it would be right to involve God with it?

___Is it all right to ask for things for ourselves?
Shouldn't our prayers always be for others?

After all, Audrey questioned, how could a Supreme God ever be interested in me and the little things I desire? Especially, with everything He has to do…holding up the world and all.

Yes, it seemed only reasonable, as Audrey gazed at the innumerable amount of stars in the nighttime sky, that with God's gigantic universe and the billions of people that need His love and attention... Audrey's wants and desires would be very small indeed to Him.

Still, Audrey continued to listen to the teaching tapes that Carla had loaned her. The minister said that there were two Kingdom's in this world, God's Kingdom and Satan's Kingdom. He quoted John 10:10 which says *"The thief comes only to steal and kill and destroy (Satan's Kingdom); I came that they may have life, and have it abundantly (God's Kingdom)."*

"It is important to become a part of God's Kingdom, especially if you are asking God for specific answers to prayer." the minister said. "You can become one of God's kids by simply asking Jesus to forgive your sins and come into your heart."

Then the minister went on to give other things to do to help insure answers to your prayers:

1) *If you are holding unforgiveness in your heart towards anyone, ask God to help you forgive. Unforgiveness can stop God's ability to answer your prayers.* Mark 11:23-26

2) *It is important to understand that God's love is unconditional, but His promises are conditional. We must obey His commandments first.* II Chronicles 7:14

3) *God is a "Faith God," and when you become His child, He expects you to live by faith. Faith is believing God more than you believe anything else.* Hebrews 11:1 & 6

4) *Faith begins like a tiny seed in your heart and will grow if you "feed" it. You feed your seed by reading the Bible and listening to God's Word, which is called the "Bread of Life."* Romans 10:17

5) Search the scriptures to find out if what you are asking for is God's will. Once you have Bible verses to back you up, boldly ask for your desires. I John 5:14-15

6) After you have prayed, rest in the fact that God has heard your prayer. Reinforce your faith by thinking about His Word and quoting His promises. John 15:7

7) Satan, of course, does not want you to receive answers to your prayers, so be prepared for a battle. You will become God's "Christian Warrior" and the battlefield will be in your mind. Satan will do whatever he can to make you doubt. He may whisper thoughts into your mind that say something like, "You were silly to think God would answer your prayers."

When those thoughts come, get ready to "fight the good fight of faith." Prepare your ammunition…God's promises in Scripture. "Throw" your ammunition at Satan's tempting thoughts by quoting God's promises and by telling Satan that you choose to believe God's Word in spite of all the discouraging circumstances. II Corinthians 10:3-5

8) Be prepared to wait for however long it takes. This is what the Bible refers to as "standing fast" in the faith. The longer you wait, the more character and strength you will develop. Romans 4:20-22

Finally, after much consideration, Audrey decided to do what the minister on the tape had said. She knelt by her bed and quietly searched her heart for any sin or unforgiveness she had not repented of, then she made her request for a stove, a refrigerator & a sink for her precious children. Audrey purposed to believe that God did want her "joy to be made full" as the verse in St. John had said.

Audrey just loved surprises! She hoped to have the little appliances in time for Jasmine and Jessica's birthday. She wanted to give them a birthday party and surprise them with the little playroom all furnished and ready to play in. Audrey looked forward to seeing the girls' eyes light up with joy over a kitchen just their size. She was certain Justin would enjoy playing with the kitchen, almost as much as the girls.

The twins' birthday was just two months away. That would give Audrey plenty of time to find the toy appliances. All the while she was doing her best to believe God would supply this desire of her heart. Besides that, Mark said they could spare $20 to apply towards the project!

The first verse Audrey found was Joshua 1:8.

This book of the law (God's Word) shall not depart from your mouth, but you shall meditate on it day and night, so that you may be careful to do according to all that is written in it. For then you will make your way prosperous, and then you will have success.

"That certainly sounds to me like God wants to bless his children," Audrey said to herself, as she noted the conditions in the verse. Then she picked up the local newspaper and started hunting through the classified section.

*****

One week passed and Audrey did not find anything in the newspapers or at local garage sales. She was not concerned, there was plenty of time. In the meantime, she was really enjoying meditating on the scriptures she was finding in God's Word.

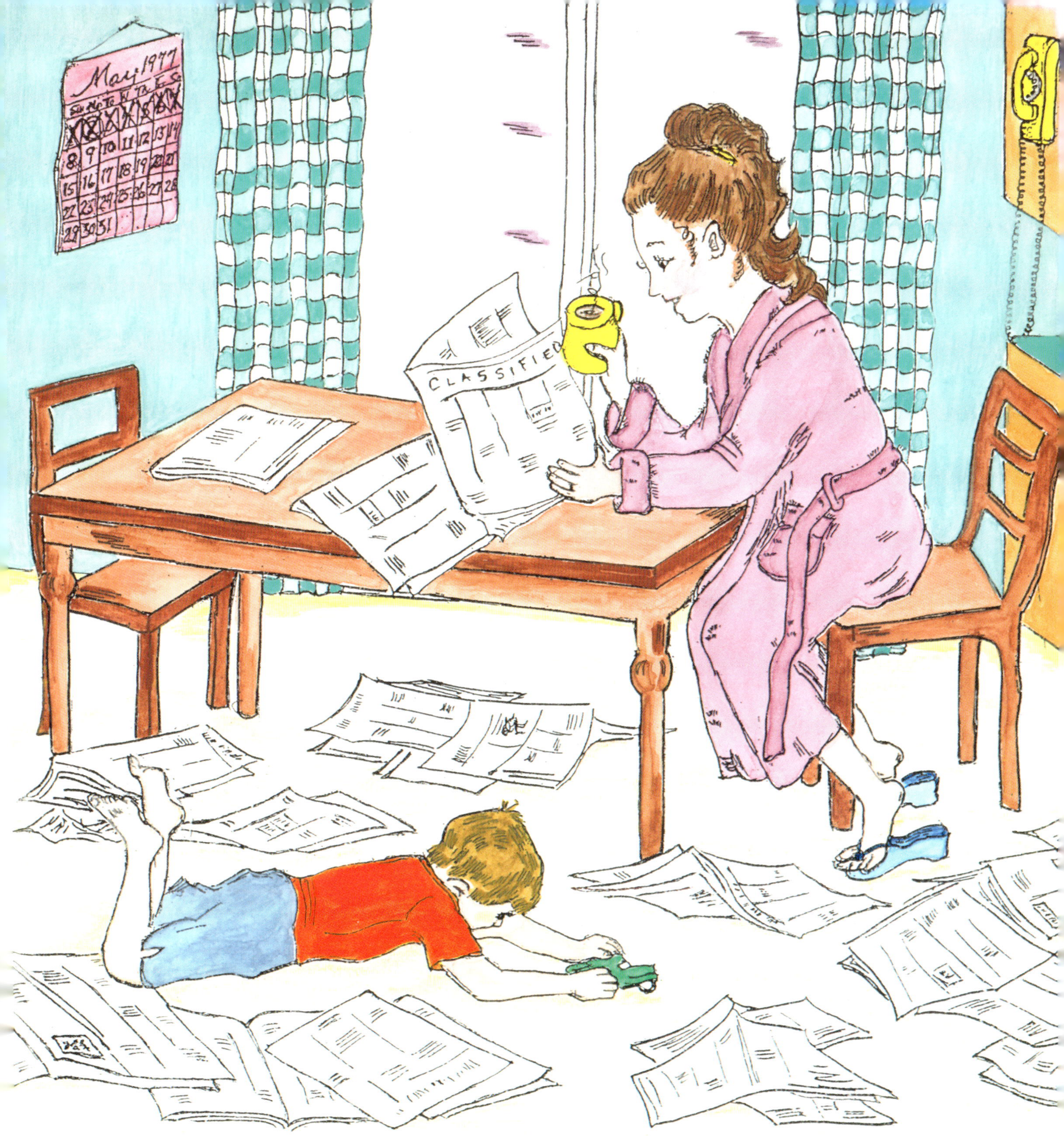
May 1977
CLASSIFIED

*E*veryday Audrey read the Bible and found encouraging verses to meditate on. Like the one in Matthew 7:7.

Ask, and it will be given to you; seek, and you will find. Knock, and it will be opened to you.

But seek first His Kingdom and His righteousness, and all these things will be added to you. Matthew 6:33

Everyday Audrey plunged into garage sale shopping and newspaper ad hunting with "great gusto!" Of course she took great pains not to let the children know what she was looking for. One must not ruin the SURPRISE!

Audrey hadn't realized the Bible was full of so many promises:

This is the confidence which we have before Him, that if we ask anything according to His will, He hears us. And if we know that He hears us in whatever we ask, we know that we have the requests which we asked from Him. I John 5:14-15

The desire of the righteous, will be granted. Proverbs 10:24b

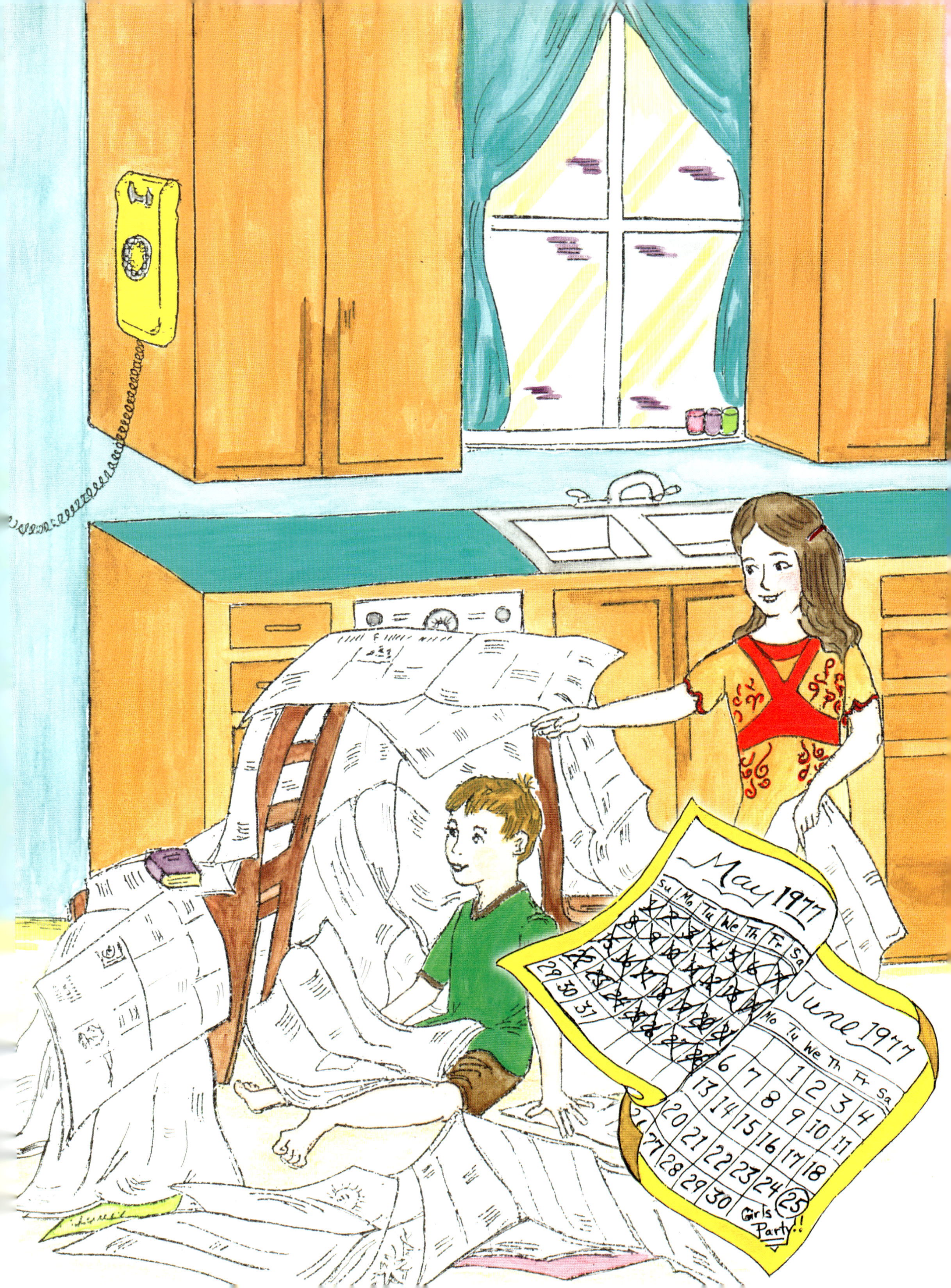
May 1977
June 1977
Girls Party!!

A udrey was learning what a comfort the scriptures could be. She thought about them a lot as she went about her day.

*Now to Him who is able to do far more **abundantly** beyond all that we ask or think, according to the power that works within us.* Ephesians 3:20

Delight yourself also in the Lord; and He will give you the desires and secret petitions of your heart. Psalms 37:4 AMP

You have given him his heart's desire, and have not withheld the request of his lips. Selah (pause and think of that)! Psalms 21:2 AMP

But as the weeks passed, not one garage sale (and Audrey visited plenty) or one newspaper ad revealed the objects of her heart's desire. Audrey had seen toy appliances many times in garage sales and newspaper ads when she wasn't anxiously looking for them, but now that she was...they were nowhere to be found!

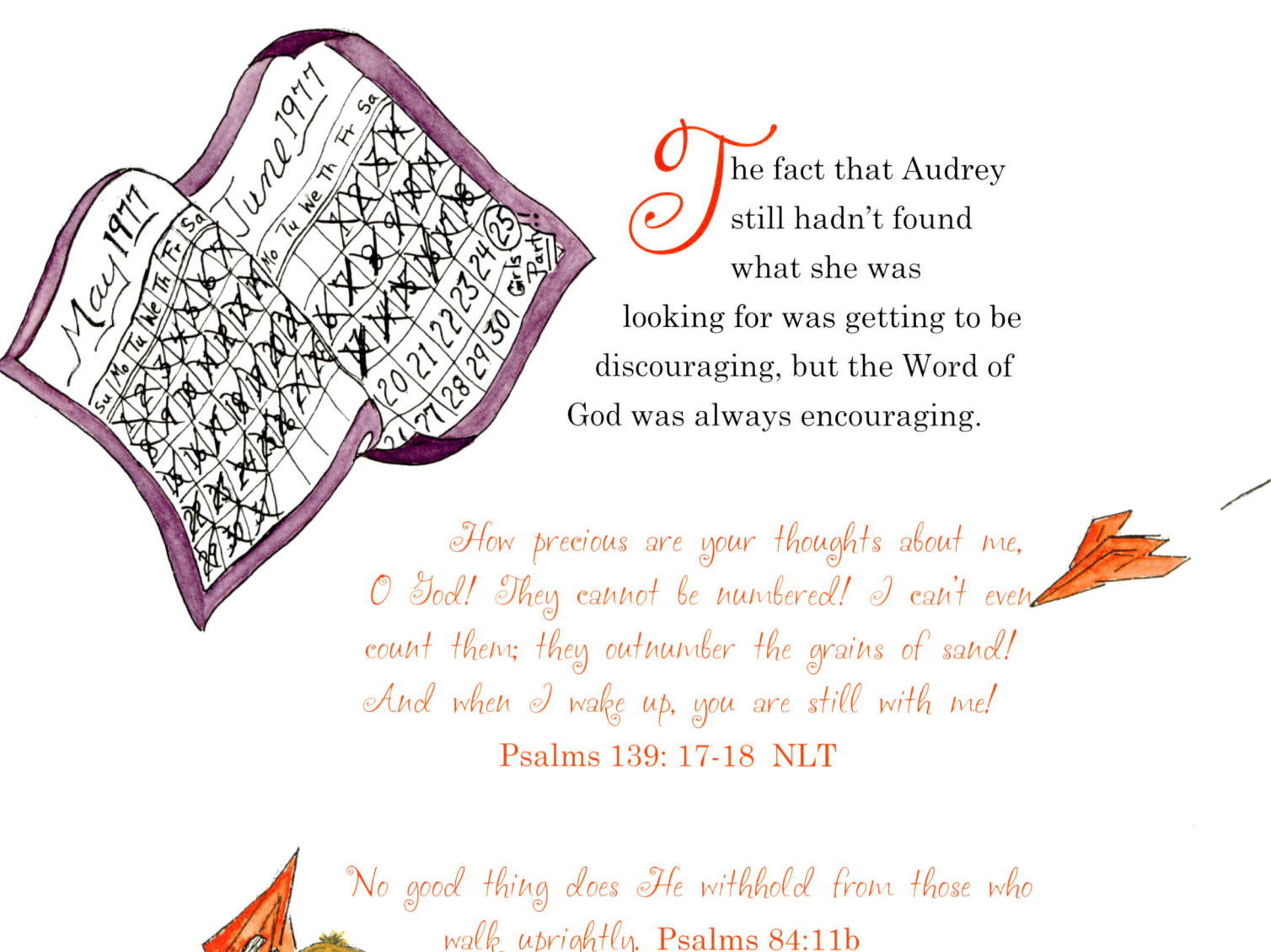

The fact that Audrey still hadn't found what she was looking for was getting to be discouraging, but the Word of God was always encouraging.

How precious are your thoughts about me, O God! They cannot be numbered! I can't even count them; they outnumber the grains of sand! And when I wake up, you are still with me!
Psalms 139: 17-18 NLT

No good thing does He withhold from those who walk uprightly. Psalms 84:11b

The weeks fell into months and Audrey began to wonder if indeed it had been foolish to pray and hope for such a thing. Finally she was down to one week before the twins' birthday party and she hadn't found a thing. Audrey's heart was sinking; she knew if she didn't find something this week, it would be too late!

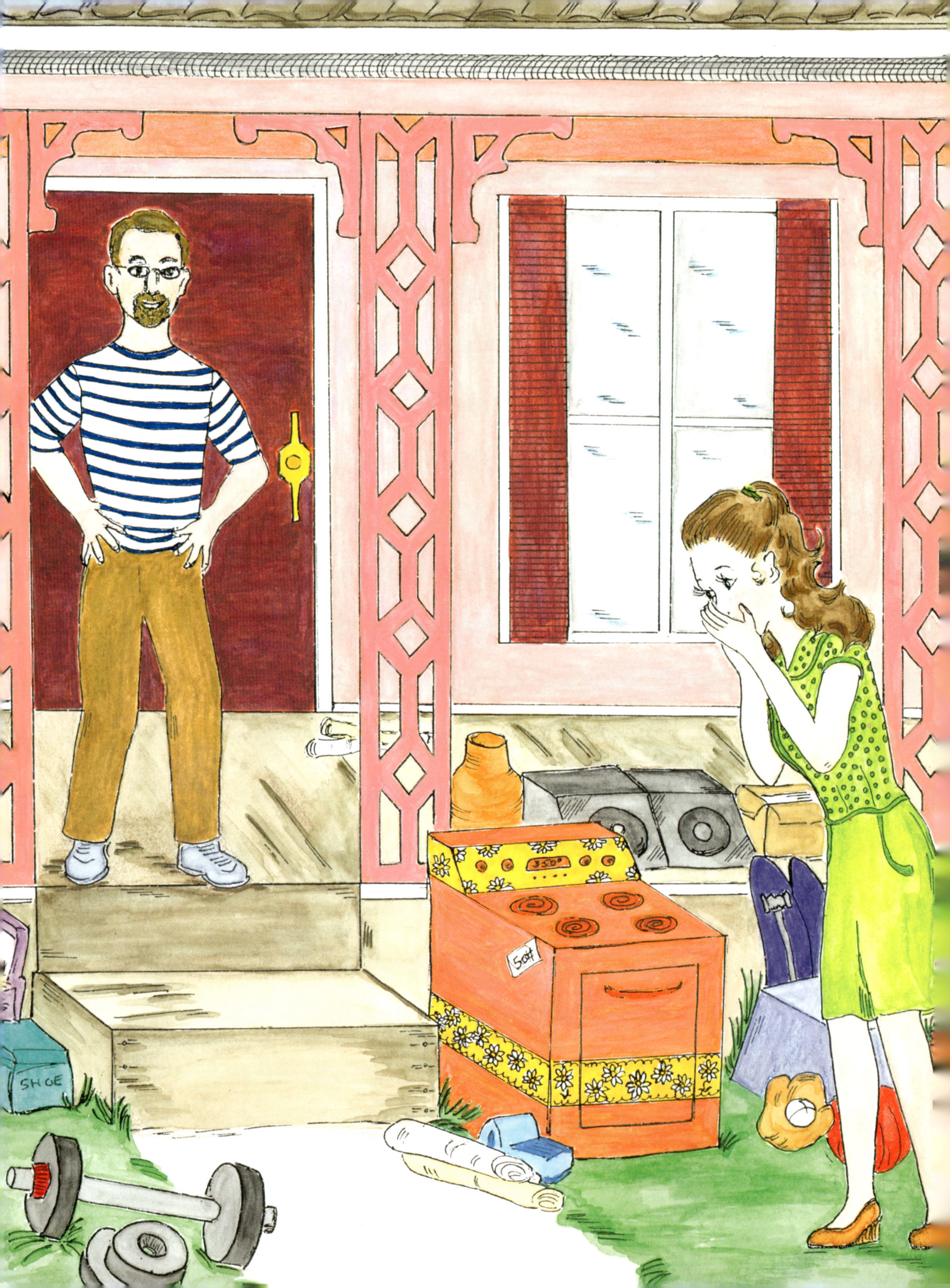
350°
50¢
SHOE

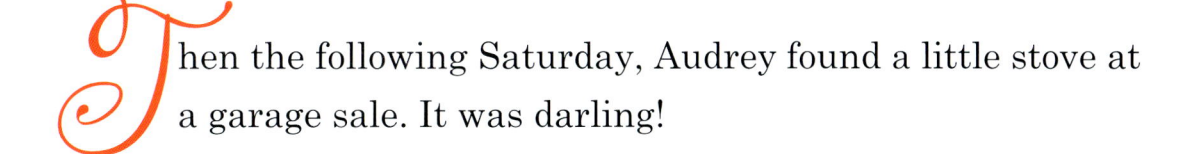

*T*hen the following Saturday, Audrey found a little stove at a garage sale. It was darling!

___It was the most deluxe model of a miniature appliance she had ever seen!

___Instead of the controls being painted on (like the cheaper models), the controls were actual knobs and the burners...real raised burners!

___The stove looked like new. There wasn't a scratch on it!

___It was bright orange, with a decorative row of little white and yellow daisies!

In all her shopping, Audrey had never seen such a darling little stove. And would you believe…it only cost 50 cents!

Just 50 cents!!

Audrey's mind was racing... with the $19.50 she had left, she could buy a new refrigerator.

For a sink, she could turn a box upside down...

and put a plastic bowl on the top of the box. That would work for the sink!

$\mathcal{A}$udrey's idea would work. No, it was not exactly what she had been dreaming of, but she was used to making do. Audrey was happy.

Of course, none of them would match, but...oh well!

When Audrey got home from the garage sale, she hid the stove in the garage among the empty packing boxes. She was certain the kids would never find it there. Then she told Mark her plan.

"Wait, don't go shopping for a refrigerator yet!" Mark said. "Let me go to the teacher's supply store on Monday. Sometimes they have little appliances like that on sale for kindergarten classes. Maybe I can find something at a discount."

Monday afternoon just dragged by. Audrey could hardly wait for Mark to get home. She was so distracted that at first she didn't notice the kids sliding down the banisters.

"Stop!" Audrey yelled, "You know you are not supposed to be doing that!" Then she added to herself, "Boy, do these kids ever need a playroom!"

*****

Mark was totally excited, when he finally got home. He was carrying two unopened boxes, instead of one.

"*Shhhh...*" Audrey whispered, "Control yourself, or you'll 'spill the beans' to the kids! Let's hide the boxes in the garage before the kids see them."

After the boxes were safely hidden, Mark excitedly told Audrey what had happened, "I went to the teacher's supply store and asked the clerk if they had a miniature refrigerator I could buy. The clerk said they did, and with the sale price it would be $16.99."

They would actually have money left over! $\$ 19.50$
$\underline{-16.99}$

The clerk started to ring up the purchase, then stopped. "Wait a minute..." he said, "We have both a refrigerator AND a sink still in the boxes in the back room. They've been sitting back there for about three years. I have no idea what they look like, but I'll let you have them BOTH for $16.99, if you like."

"Yes," Mark told the clerk, "I would like that *very much!*"

𝒜udrey could hardly wait for the kids to go to bed that night so she and Mark could open the boxes. After the kids were finally in bed, Audrey received her own personal revelation of God's love.

When Audrey and Mark opened the boxes and began to put the appliances together, they found they were deluxe toy models.

___The refrigerator had real handles on it, just like the real knobs and burners on the stove.

___The sink had a container where water could be stored, so that when you turned the real knobs, water would pour out!

The thing that thrilled Audrey the most, however, was that God had answered her "secret" desire.

They were both orange...

with a decorative row of little white and yellow daisies.

All three matched perfectly!

$\mathcal{T}$he morning of the birthday party, Audrey and Mark surprised the girls by blindfolding them and leading them into their new playroom. Sure enough, their eyes lit up with joy, especially at the sight of the new "state of the art" kitchen with the "ultra modern and stylish" stove, refrigerator, and sink.

All of the guests who came to the party were served a pretend dinner cooked in Jasmine & Jessica's new kitchen, with Justin being the chief waiter. No one was the least bit interested in real birthday cake! Not for quite awhile…that is.

As Audrey watched the happy sight, she could hardly contain the joy welling up within her. Not only was she joyful about seeing the kids so happy with their new playroom and appliances, but she was thrilled about her new revelation of God's love. Audrey was awestruck that God cared that much about three little toy appliances...because it mattered so much to her!

She could hardly fathom that *three years before she had even asked* God had them set aside for her!

It was amazing to realize that God has such a heart for His children! Just as Audrey wanted more than anything to fix up the playroom for her children… to see the joy in their eyes!

So her Heavenly Father had a special surprise for Audrey… so that He could see the joy in hers!

After the last piece of real birthday cake had been served and the guests had gone home, Audrey and Mark gathered the children together and told them the story of how their special playroom came to be. How it happened that their Mom and Dad were able to give them the new "state of the art" kitchen appliances.

Then everyone knelt and thanked God for *"His Special Surprises!"*

Now who do you think surprised who!?!